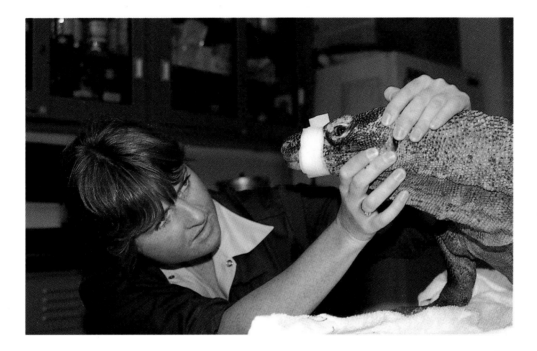

ZOO WORLD

THE WORK OF THE
ZOO DOCTORS
AT THE SAN DIEGO ZOO

BY GEORGEANNE IRVINE

SIMON & SCHUSTER BOOKS FOR YOUNG READERS
Published by Simon & Schuster
New York · London · Toronto · Sydney · Tokyo · Singapore

With love to my Baby Boo Bradley Berlinger, and to Mikey and
Buster, who have had their share of visits to the veterinarian.

ACKNOWLEDGMENTS
My sincerest thanks to Dr. Don Janssen, Dr. Mike Loomis, Dr. Jim Oosterhuis,
Dr. Amy Shima, Dr. Jeff Zuba, Dr. Susanne Abildgaard Anderson, Kim Williams
and the rest of the San Diego Zoo and Wild Animal Park hospital staff for
helping me teach children about veterinary care and for dedicating your lives
to animal health. In addition, thank you to Ron Garrison, Kathy Marmack,
Alan Benjamin, Dorothy Irvine, Victoria Garrison, Ken Kelley, Alison Holland
and Lise Christensen for making this book a reality.

PHOTO CREDITS
Ron Garrison: front cover; endsheets; back cover top right
and lower left; 5; 6; 9; 10; 11; 12; 13; 14; 15; 16; 17; 18;
19; 20 lower; 21; 22; 23; 24; 25; 26 top left; 27; 28; 29; 30; 31;
32; 33; 34; 35; 36; 37; 40; 41 lower; 42; 43. Georgeanne Irvine:
26 top right and lower; 38; 39. Craig Racicot: back cover top
left and lower right. Ken Kelley: 41 top. John Mitchell: 20 top.

SIMON & SCHUSTER
BOOKS FOR YOUNG READERS
Simon & Schuster Building
Rockefeller Center
1230 Avenue of the Americas
New York, New York 10020
Copyright © 1991 by the Zoological Society
of San Diego and Georgeanne Irvine
All rights reserved including the right
of reproduction in whole or in part in any form.
SIMON & SCHUSTER BOOKS FOR YOUNG READERS
is a trademark of Simon & Schuster.
Designed by Kathleen Westray
Manufactured in the United States of America
10 9 8 7 6 5 4 3 2 1

Library of Congress Cataloging-in-Publication Data
Irvine, Georgeanne.
The work of the zoo doctors at the San Diego Zoo /
by Georgeanne Irvine.
p.   cm.
Summary: Describes the work of the veterinarians at the
San Diego Zoo as they treat sick and injured animals and work
to save species through conservation and breeding programs.
1. Zoo veterinarians—Juvenile literature.   2. Zoo veterinarians—
California—San Diego—Juvenile literature.   3. San Diego Zoo—
Juvenile literature.   [1. Zoo veterinarians.   2. San Diego Zoo.
3. Occupations.]   I. Title
SF995.85.I78   1991
636.089'069—dc20   90-25760   CIP   AC
ISBN 0-671-73921-2

CONTENTS

KEN ALLEN, the most popular orangutan at the San Diego Zoo, had a doctor's appointment he just couldn't miss. The shaggy red-haired ape, a famous escape artist who had scaled the walls of his exhibit many times over the years, was due for his yearly physical with the Zoo's veterinarians.

To the keepers who cared for him, Ken Allen seemed to be in good health. He ate well, had a clear nose and eyes, and continually explored every corner of his enclosure, looking for opportunities to climb out. A small wart above Ken Allen's nose, though, had been growing larger, and the keepers wanted the veterinarians to examine it. Because Ken Allen is a rare animal, a member of an endangered species native to the island of Borneo, it was especially important to look for and check anything unusual.

Dr. Amy Shima, a Zoo veterinarian, visited Ken Allen in his sleeping area to prepare him for the short trip to the hospital. Using a blow dart from outside the bars, she tranquilized the orangutan with a drug. He threw a handful of hay at Dr. Shima as he lay down to sleep.

Ken Allen was wheeled on a gurney to the veterinary van for the ride to the hospital. Dr. Shima accompanied her patient.

At the hospital, other veterinarians, plus keepers and animal health technicians (nurses for animals), prepared for Ken Allen's arrival.

Also waiting were two doctors who normally dealt with human patients. One was an anesthesiologist, Dr. Stan Perkins. His job was to give Ken Allen proper doses of a special gas in order to make sure he stayed asleep, and to monitor his heart and breathing rates. The other doctor, Doug Cassat, was a dentist who was standing by in case Ken Allen needed dental work. The orangutan had a history of teeth problems.

The plan was to keep Ken Allen anesthetized for as short a time as possible, since there is always a certain amount of risk when putting an animal, or even a human, to sleep with drugs.

First, Ken Allen was weighed on a huge outdoor scale. His weight, 227 pounds, was close to what he had weighed the previous year. This

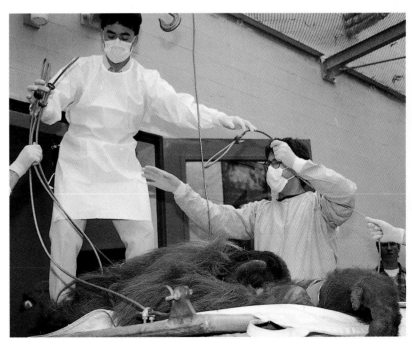

pleased the veterinarians and keepers because significant weight loss or gain can indicate medical problems.

Next, he was moved into an examining room, where many things happened at once. While the dentist examined Ken Allen's mouth and took X-rays of his teeth, the Zoo veterinarians and hospital staff drew blood samples, listened to Ken Allen's heart and lungs, measured his blood pressure, inspected his skin, and checked his joints and muscles. An instrument called an electrocardiograph, or ECG machine, gave a detailed printout of Ken Allen's heart activity.

The dentist found that Ken Allen had a rotten tooth that had to be pulled. It was surprising that the orangutan hadn't been acting cranky toward his keepers and orangutan roommates, because the decayed tooth had probably caused him a lot of pain. Dr. Cassat removed the tooth in sections because it had several roots.

After the orangutan's dental work was completed, the Zoo's veterinary resident, Dr. Jeff Zuba, checked the wart above Ken Allen's nose. (A resident is someone who is receiving two more years of specialized training with exotic animals.) The wart had to be removed, too, because

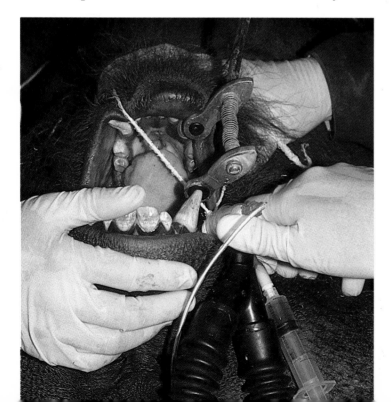
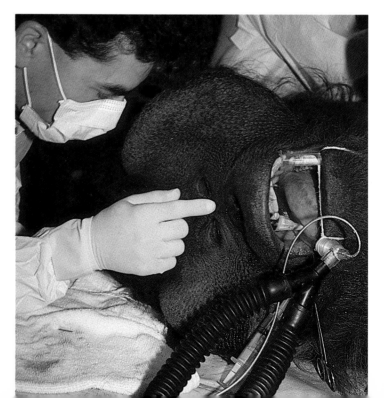

it could become a problem if it grew any larger. While Dr. Zuba performed the surgery, animal health technician Kim Williams brushed the tangles, dirt, and straw out of Ken Allen's long red hair with a metal comb.

A chest X-ray was the last part of the physical. The X-ray could detect things like a lung disease called tuberculosis or an enlarged heart. It is tricky to X-ray the chest of a sleeping animal as large as Ken Allen. The veterinarians sat him down on the floor of the X-ray room with his back against a panel that held the X-ray film. His arms were raised above his head and held in place with ropes. Then the X-ray machine was wheeled over to him. Ken Allen created a minor stir when he growled and began to wake up during his X-ray. Dr. Perkins, the anesthesiologist, hurried to give him a bit more gas, which put him to sleep again.

Because Ken Allen was found to be in excellent health, his recovery room for the rest of the day was his own sleeping area, not the hospital. The following morning, Ken Allen was up to his usual antics in his outdoor enclosure. He ambled around his pen, tossed clumps of dirt and grass toward Zoo visitors who were watching him, and climbed onto his giant jungle gym with his roommates. The shaggy orangutan was feeling fine!

13

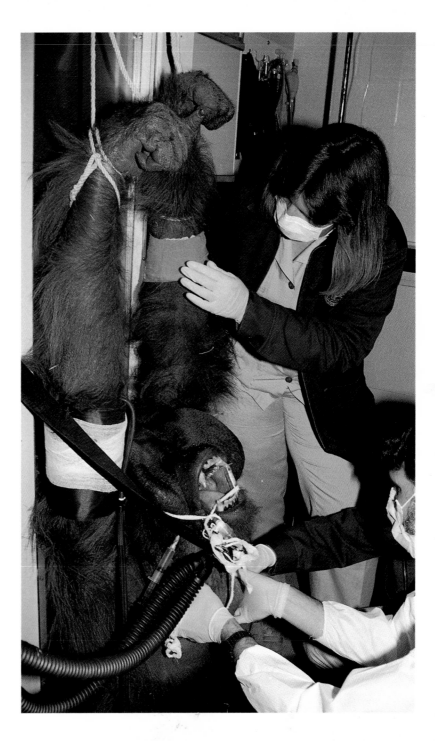

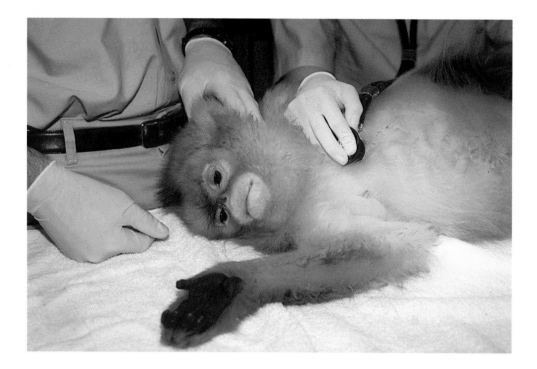

K EN ALLEN IS only one of the thousands of animal patients that the veterinarians at the San Diego Zoo and its sister facility, the San Diego Wild Animal Park, care for each year. With so much of the earth's precious wildlife facing extinction because of habitat destruction and poaching, zoos like those in San Diego are working to save many endangered species.

The world-famous San Diego Zoo and Wild Animal Park are home to over seven thousand exotic and rare birds, mammals, and reptiles. The veterinarians, who are the doctors for the Zoo and Park, are responsible for maintaining every animal's health.

With so many kinds of animals to treat, each day is challenging and interesting. The veteri-

14

narians must have knowledge of a wide range of animals, from the tiniest hummingbird to an enormous elephant—and they constantly learn new things about their patients.

The veterinarians' job is difficult because the animals cannot tell them how they feel or where it hurts. Animals are very good at hiding their illnesses since in the wild, being sick is a sign of weakness. Ken Allen's rotten tooth most likely bothered him, but he never showed signs of being in pain. Other animals might not show any symptoms of illness yet be close to death.

The veterinarians work closely with the keepers, who care for the animals daily. If the keepers notice anything unusual about an animal—like the wart above Ken Allen's nose that started growing larger, a swollen foot on an Amur cat, or perhaps a chameleon that has stopped eating its crickets—they alert the veterinarians.

The veterinarians at the Zoo and Wild Animal Park spend most of their time treating the sick or injured animals that need attention right away. A typical daily patient list could include a slow loris with a bite wound on its back, a Chinese newt with a skin infection, a newborn orangutan whose mother has rejected it, a fruit bat that has been chewing on its wing, or a clouded leopard with a flea problem.

15

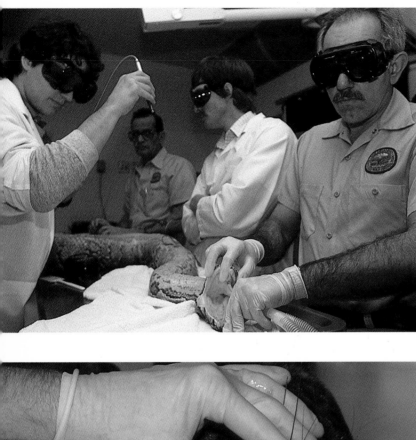

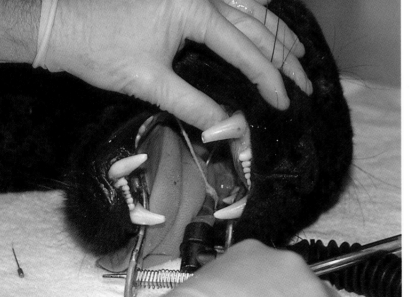

Sick and injured animals aren't the most cooperative patients. A lion or leopard that's not feeling well can be doubly dangerous. Years ago, zoo veterinarians had a difficult time treating many animals because they didn't have the proper drugs to put the animals to sleep. To trim the hooves on a large antelope or perform surgery on a lion, keepers had to lasso the animal and tie it up so the veterinarians could work on it. This put the doctors, keepers, and animal in jeopardy. Ken Allen could never have had such a thorough physical had he been awake the whole time.

Only since the late 1960s have zoo veterinarians had adequate drugs for anesthetizing and restraining their patients. Now that they do, veterinary care has advanced a great deal. It is now possible to perform laser surgery on a python to remove cancerous tumors from the roof of its mouth or to do a root canal on a tiger or jaguar.

Although the veterinarians spend a major part of their day treating sick and injured animals, they consider the practice of preventive medicine to be most important. Preventive medicine means doing things for animals that will keep them healthy and well.

Giving Ken Allen a yearly medical checkup is preventive, as was removing his wart before it became a problem. Vaccinating North Chinese leopard cubs against a number of cat diseases or providing a gorilla troop with daily vitamins helps keep those animals healthy. Other preventive measures include examining newborn animals like a Sichuan takin, a cheetah cub, or a baby pudu to make sure they are drinking their mother's milk and do not have birth defects.

Preventing the spread of life-threatening and contagious diseases is important, too. All animals that are brought to the Zoo and Wild Animal Park must spend at least thirty days in quarantine. This gives the veterinarians a chance to make sure the new animals are not ill. The veterinarians also give the new animals complete physicals, help them adjust to diet changes, and sometimes tatoo them for identification purposes.

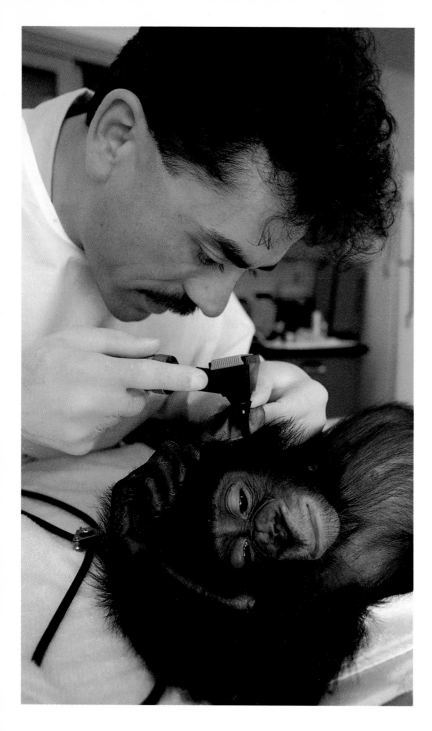

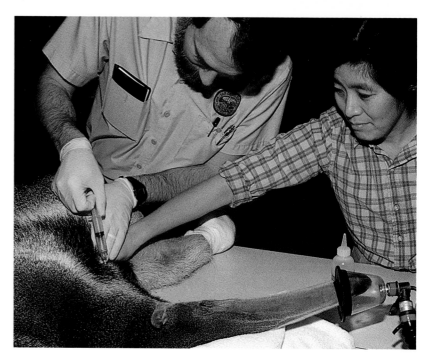

Animals that are transferred from the Zoo or Park to new homes are also examined. Whether it is a pair of anteaters going to the Philadelphia Zoo or a pygmy chimpanzee being moved from the Zoo to the Wild Animal Park, the animals are given preshipment exams. Medical records are sent with the animals to their new homes.

When animals die, special veterinarians called pathologists try to figure out the causes of their death. A lot can be learned about caring for living animals by studying these reports. When Ralph the toucan died, a pathologist determined that he had had too much iron in his diet. As a result,

the amount of blueberries, dates, and raisins in the other toucans' meals was reduced because those fruits contained a lot of iron.

The Zoo's hospital is designed especially for animals. The surgery, X-ray, and treatment rooms and laboratories look similar to those in a hospital for humans. In some of the recovery rooms, however, the walls and floors are padded so that fragile animals like impalas and Cuvier's gazelles won't hurt themselves when they are waking up from the anesthesia. Stalls, barns, and cages for housing many different patients—from sea lions to shoebill storks to Sumatran rhinoceroses—

surround the hospital. The Zoo pharmacy stocks many kinds of medicines, plus tranquilizer guns, blow darts, and nets for catching animals. The Wild Animal Park has a well-equipped hospital, too, although it is smaller than the Zoo's.

To make house calls around the Zoo and Wild Animal Park, the veterinarians travel in a special truck, which is like a hospital on wheels. In the back of the truck are compartments for all the things the veterinarians need to treat animals in their own enclosures.

With so many animals to care for, the veterinarians at the Zoo and the Park meet with the

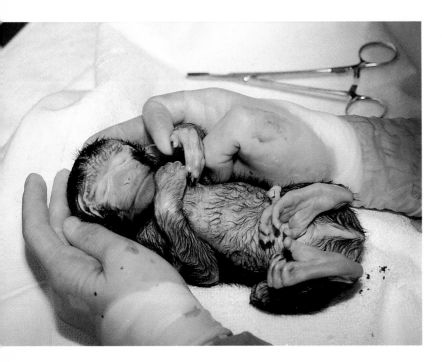

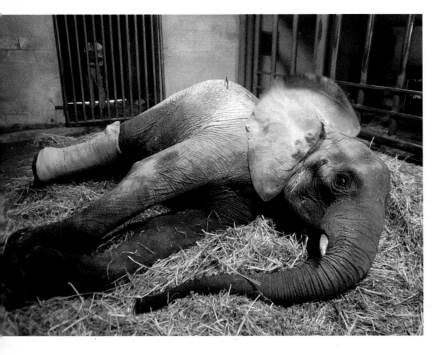

hospital staff every morning to organize their day. Most major operations and exams are scheduled. A medical checkup for an animal like Ken Allen would be planned days in advance, as would surgery called a Caesarean section to help a Celebes crested macaque deliver a baby.

The veterinarian's schedule, however, can change when there is an animal emergency, such as the escape of a Malayan sun bear that must be tranquilized, captured, and returned to its enclosure. On one busy day, Dr. Amy Shima was called upon to save the life of a drowning baby Baird's tapir that had been born in a pond. As Lola, the newborn tapir, was rushed to the Zoo hospital, Dr. Shima got her heart beating again by doing cardiopulmonary resuscitation (CPR), which involved pushing up and down on Lola's chest. At the hospital, Dr. Shima put an oxygen tube down Lola's windpipe and pumped air into the baby tapir's lungs to get her to breathe. Lola survived and was hand raised in the Children's Zoo nursery.

There are three veterinarians at the San Diego Zoo, three veterinarians at the San Diego Wild Animal Park, and a veterinary resident. They all play an important role in preserving the many rare and endangered species at the Zoo, the Wild Animal Park, and around the world.

A Day with Dr. O

THE GRAY SPRING morning was still cool as the Wild Animal Park's chief veterinarian, Dr. Jim Oosterhuis, met with his staff to discuss the schedule for the day. Dr. O, as everyone calls him, scanned an animal examination calendar and keeper reports, then made a list of the animals that needed attention that day. Dr. O and the

other two veterinarians, Dr. Phil Ensley and Dr. Jack Allen, each had many animals to examine.

Before making his first house call at the Park's animal care center, where orphaned and sick baby animals are hand raised, Dr. O gathered the medicines he would need from the hospital pharmacy. Then he drove to the care center in the veterinary truck with animal health technician Amy Chaddock. Their first patient was a one-month-

old Thompson's gazelle with an eye injury. This was Dr. O's second visit to the gazelle, whose injury may have been caused by a piece of hay or a small pebble scraping its eye. While keeper Gail Thurston held the young gazelle, Dr. O put a solution in the animal's eye that would help the veterinarian see the injury more clearly. Dr. O looked into the gazelle's eye, first with a blue light, then with an instrument called an opthalmoscope. The injury appeared to be healing, but Dr. O asked Gail to medicate the eye with antibiotic eyedrops three times daily until he could examine it again in a few days.

Also at the care center was a young female

sitatunga with an upset stomach. Dr. O prescribed Pepto-Bismol® to settle her stomach.

In the 125-acre East Africa enclosure, Dr. O shot a tranquilizer dart into a female Roosevelt's gazelle. Keepers carried the gazelle into a protective pen called a boma, where Dr. O examined her and took a blood sample. Because the animal was thinner than the other gazelles, Dr. O thought that perhaps she wasn't eating well. He asked the keepers to hold her in the boma for a few weeks so she could be watched.

looked closely at her abscess using binoculars. The following day, he would have to anesthetize Goalpara to drain and treat the abscess again.

At the okapi barn, Dr. O checked Kelle, a five-month-old okapi who had recently had surgery to straighten her knock-kneed legs. Dr. O looked at Kelle's legs from different angles, but it was still too soon to tell whether the surgery had corrected her problem adequately.

A visit to the huge Southern Africa exhibit was next. Keeper Steve Coat joined Dr. O to examine a two-day-old gemsbok calf whose mother wasn't paying much attention to it. The cream-colored calf had been lying quietly in the sand for most of the morning. Often, antelope mothers hide their babies while they graze, but they usually come back so the calves can nurse. The gemsbok mother, however, seemed to be neglecting her baby.

Dr. O gave the baby an overall health checkup, then took a blood sample that would be analyzed to see whether the calf had been nursing. If the baby didn't have milk in its system, it would have to go to the animal care center to be hand raised. Before Dr. O left, he told Steve to carry the calf to a shady spot if the gray skies turned sunny.

By now it was midday, and Dr. O had to get back to the Park hospital to examine more ani-

The next patient was Goalpara, a three-and-a-half-year-old Indian rhinoceros with an abscess on her side. She was staying in an Asian Plains enclosure boma with Gainda, another Indian rhino, who was there to keep her company. Dr. O had already treated the sore, so he examined Goalpara from a walkway above the boma. Because he could not enter the enclosure with the large rhino while she was awake, Dr. O

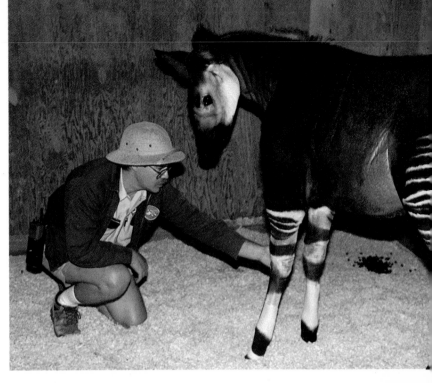

mals. He also had to check on Connie, a pregnant Asian elephant who was due to give birth in a few weeks. After that, there were more keeper reports to go over, animal medical records to fill out and enter into the computer, several articles on exotic animal health to read, and numerous phone calls to return. And, somewhere in between all these things, Dr. O would try to find time to eat his lunch.

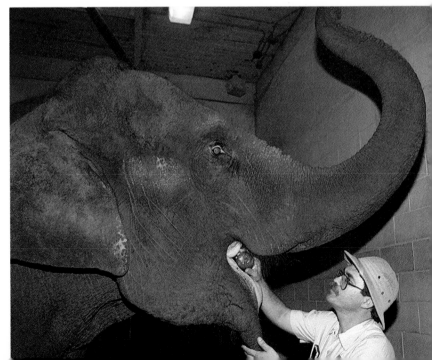

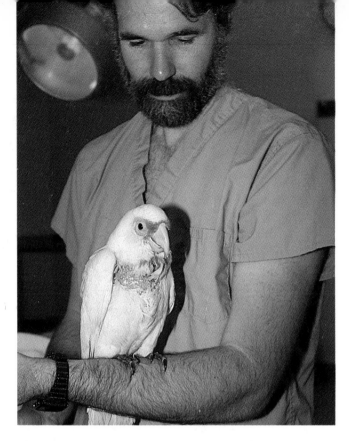

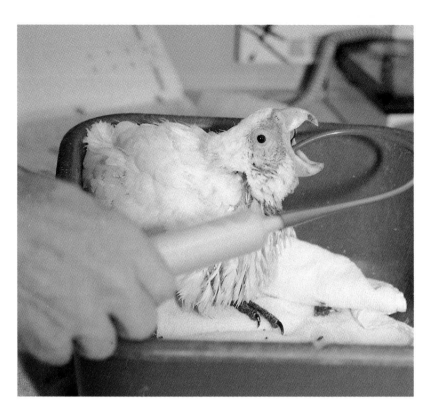

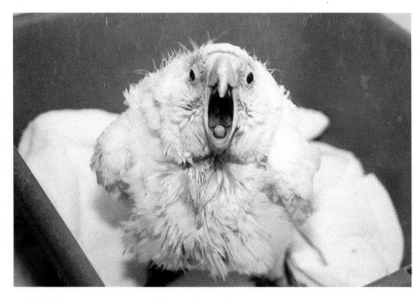

A Black Light Exam

A YOUNG SLENDER-BILLED cockatoo squawked loudly as Dr. Mike Loomis gently carried him from his cage at the Zoo's bird hatchery to a counter where he could be examined. The chick's crop, which is a muscular throat sac that stores food before it is digested, had not emptied for three days. This meant that a lot of the bird's food was not being digested, and could decay and infect the small cockatoo.

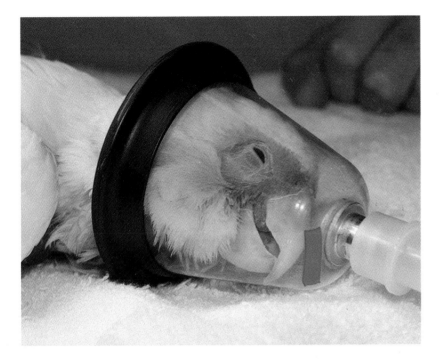
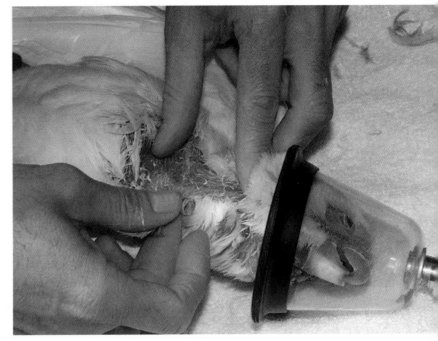

Inserting a thin rubber tube in the bird's mouth, Dr. Loomis drained the cockatoo's crop. He prescribed antibiotics for the bird, to be given twice a day in its food, and asked the keepers to report to him on the cockatoo's condition.

Several days later, the keepers noticed food leaking from the young bird's crop. A hole in the crop was discovered that Dr. Loomis would have to repair by surgery.

At the Zoo hospital, a mask was put over the slender-billed cockatoo's face and the bird was anesthetized with gas. To prepare the bird for surgery, Dr. Loomis plucked the feathers around the chick's crop area. He then stitched up the hole. Somehow the crop had been injured, which was why it had not drained. Once the skin around the injury died, it had flaked off, making the hole.

Three weeks after the surgery, the cockatoo was back at the hospital because keepers thought it had developed more holes in its crop. Lots of food had dribbled onto the bird's feathers.

Once again Dr. Loomis anesthetized the cockatoo. Then, using a needle, he injected a fluorescent dye into a vein in the bird's wing. The Zoo veterinarian waited a few minutes, turned out the lights in the surgery room, and shined a special black light over the bird. Under the black light's purple glow, the cockatoo's healthy skin became a fluorescent yellow. If there were any holes in the crop, they would appear as dark

areas. This is because the fluorescent dye flows through the bloodstream only to healthy skin.

Dr. Loomis was pleased to find that the cockatoo's crop had no new holes in it where food could seep out. When the bird was returned to the keepers, Dr. Loomis smiled as he told them that the young slender-billed cockatoo most likely had food on its feathers because it had become a messy eater.

A Fishy Dental Checkup

CORKY THE HARBOR SEAL, a star in the Zoo's Animal Chit-Chat Show, always smelled a little fishy since he ate mackerel, butterfish, and squid all day long. His trainers had noticed, however, that in the past couple of weeks, his breath had a new and unusual odor, and that his gums were bleeding.

It was difficult to examine Corky's mouth closely, but the symptoms indicated that he needed a dental examination at the Zoo hospital. Trainer Kathy Marmack lured Corky into a crate with a big mackerel. Going to the hospital was an unusual activity that made Corky nervous because the twelve-year-old harbor seal was blind. Performing in daily shows was easy for him because he knew his routine by memory, but he wasn't used to traveling in a crate.

Zoo veterinarian Dr. Don Janssen waited for Corky with veterinarian Dr. Jim McBain and keeper Dee Cross from the aquatic park, Sea World. They had been asked to assist with Corky's exam. Seals are very difficult to anesthetize because they have sensitive breathing systems and the Sea World people have had more experience with seals than the Zoo's veterinarians.

Keeper Dee netted Corky to prevent him from biting anyone. He then straddled the seal to hold him in place while the veterinarians tried to anesthetize him. They used a large gas mask made from a cutout bleach bottle. Corky was so frightened, however, that Dr. Janssen gave him a shot to calm him down. Trainer Kathy talked soothingly to Corky. Her familiar voice helped put him at ease.

Corky resisted the anesthesia at first by holding

his breath for five minutes and not breathing in the gas. Seals can hold their breath for long periods of time because they swim underwater to hunt for fish.

Finally, Corky fell asleep, and Dr. Janssen was able to check his mouth. It turned out that the odor was caused by several decayed teeth that had crumbled because they were so rotten. Corky's other teeth were thick with tartar, which caused his gums to bleed. Dr. Janssen pulled eight of the seal's teeth, cleaned the others by scraping off the tartar, and X-rayed his mouth.

While Dr. Janssen worked, the animal health technicians placed wet towels on Corky's flippers

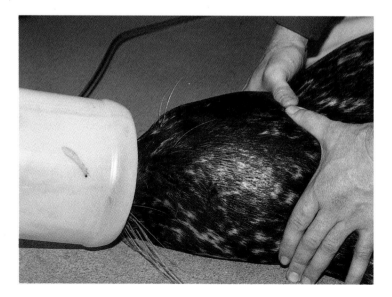

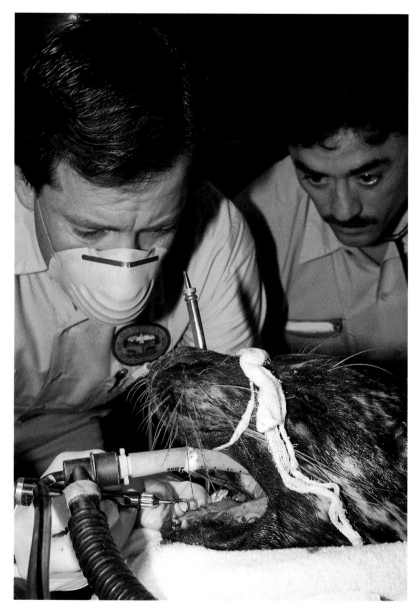

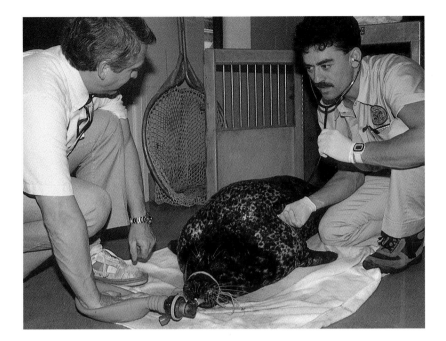

and bags of ice on his tail. This was done to keep the harbor seal cool. Marine mammals like Corky can easily overheat when they are out of the water.

During the exam, a tube pumped oxygen to Corky's lungs. Seals are voluntary breathers, which means that they must think about every breath they take. Because Corky was under anesthesia, he might not have breathed on his own and could have died if he had not been given oxygen.

After a complete health checkup, which even included trimming Corky's toenails, he slowly awakened from the anesthesia, with trainer Kathy by his side. Dr. McBain helped Corky breathe as he woke up by pumping air into him with an instrument called an Ambu-bag.

When Corky was well enough to perform in the Animal Chit-Chat Show a few days later, Kathy began teaching him a new activity. She wanted him to be able to open his mouth on command. This would make it a lot easier for her to keep a watchful eye on Corky's teeth and gums in the future.

A Baby Giraffe Emergency

VISITORS TO the San Diego Zoo were fascinated as they watched the birth of a rare Masai giraffe just before closing time on a warm summer evening.

Early the next day, the unsteady newborn, who was named Jean, fell into the shallow moat surrounding her enclosure. Keepers rescued the calf and carried her into the giraffe barn, where they noticed she had a swollen front ankle.

A short time later, Dr. Amy Shima arrived to give Jean a routine "new baby check" and to examine her ankle. Several keepers held the 75-pound, 5-foot, 6-inch-tall calf still while Dr. Shima listened to her heart and lungs, took her temperature, drew blood samples, and checked her overall condition, including her ankle. Dr. Shima said that the ankle was sprained and bandaged it for support. Within a few days, the swelling was gone and Jean was galloping around the giraffe enclosure with her mother to the delight of Zoo visitors.

When Jean was four months old, she developed a new problem that concerned the keepers and veterinarians. For some unknown reason, the hock area of one of her back legs was swollen, and Jean was limping. The veterinarians moni-

tored her leg every day for several weeks to see if the swelling went down on its own.

Because her leg didn't get better, it had to be X-rayed. Normally, large animals like giraffes, elephants, and rhinoceroses are too big to go to the hospital, so the X-ray equipment is brought to them. Jean was still small enough, however—

9 feet tall and 357 pounds—to be moved to the hospital. The keepers padded a trailer with bed mattresses to transport her there safely.

When Jean arrived, she was anesthetized before she was moved from the trailer to the X-ray room. Her long neck was strapped to a splint for support.

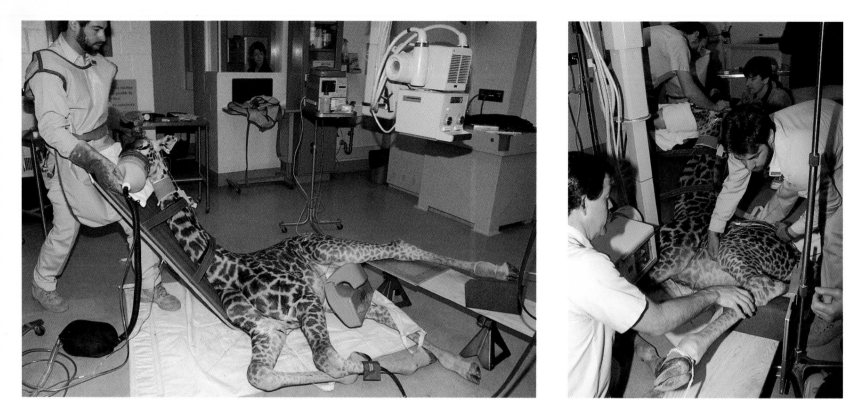

Dr. Don Janssen stretched out Jean's leg and tied it in place for the X-ray because it was important for the leg to stay still. After an animal health technician developed the X-rays, Dr. Janssen and the other veterinarians studied them. Although the X-rays were difficult to read, they seemed to show that Jean's leg was fractured. To get another opinion, the veterinarians sent the pictures to another doctor, called a radiologist, who specialized in X-rays. They also wanted a surgeon to look at the X-rays and to advise them on how to treat the injury. Since the veterinarians could not treat Jean yet, they felt she would be under less stress with her mother, and moved her back to the giraffe enclosure.

The cause of Jean's hock problem wasn't clear to the radiologist or surgeon, either. They thought that Jean's hock was fractured, but they wanted to study additional X-rays showing different views of her leg.

A few weeks later, Jean was taken back to the Zoo hospital for more X-rays. These pictures clearly showed that a small bone was fractured and chipped, and that this was causing the hock to swell. Jean would need surgery to remove the chip and correct the problem.

The surgery was scheduled for the following month. Once again, Jean rode to the hospital in the padded trailer. The surgeon, Dr. Dan Evans, helped the Zoo veterinarians with the delicate operation. It was successful. The doctors felt sure that when Jean's hock healed, it would not bother her anymore.

But as Jean woke up from the anesthesia and was being loaded into the trailer, something tragic happened: Her heart stopped beating. The veterinarians tried everything they could to revive her, but baby Jean was dead.

The veterinarians, keepers, and hospital staff were upset, of course, by Jean's death, which had been caused by an uncommon reaction to the anesthesia. They had done their best and lost. However, what they learned through their many months of dealing with Jean was valuable information that would be useful in treating giraffes and other animals with similar leg problems.

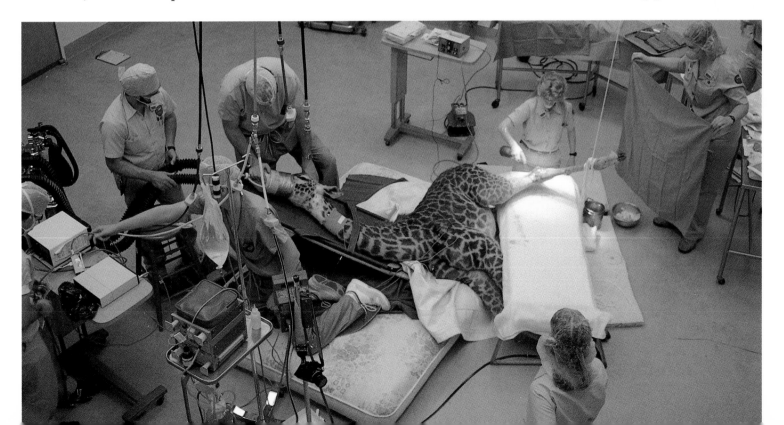

Hide It in an Oreo

TO GET ZULEIKA, a rare Hartmann's mountain zebra, to take a dose of worming medicine every few months, the Zoo veterinarians and Animal Chit-Chat Show trainer Kathy Marmack had to be very creative...and very sneaky.

Zuleika is not fond of the veterinarians who give her the shots that she dislikes. She is even less fond of the white, pasty medicine that Dr. Don Janssen prescribes for her every three months to prevent her intestines from becoming infected with worms. Because Dr. Janssen could not get close to skittish Zuleika, he instructed trainer Kathy to give her the medicine.

The first time Kathy medicated Zuleika, she petted and scratched the zebra while she quickly squirted medicine from a syringe into Zuleika's mouth. Zuleika was taken by surprise and swallowed it. A few months later, Kathy tried the same method again. This time, Zuleika spit out every drop of medicine. The zebra seemed to hate the taste of it.

Zuleika learned to recognize the syringe by sight and smell. When it came time for her dose of worming medicine, the alert zebra wouldn't let Kathy near her.

Because it was important to Zuleika's health

that she take the awful-tasting medicine, Kathy came up with a new idea. She would trick Zuleika by hiding her medicine in some new food treats. Kathy discussed her plan with Dr. Janssen, who thought it might work.

An Oreo™ cookie test was first. Kathy scraped the frosting from the inside of a couple of Oreos™, substituting the white medicine. After she had

fed Zuleika several ordinary Oreos™ filled with frosting, Kathy slipped the medicated ones into the zebra's mouth and she swallowed those, too. Zuleika had been tricked into taking her medicine.

Zuleika was wiser than Kathy imagined, though. A few months later, when Kathy tried the Oreo™ trick again, Zuleika ignored the cookies.

Kathy solved that problem, however, by alternating food treats containing Zuleika's medicine.

Now, whenever Kathy gives Zuleika her worming medicine, she might hide it in blueberry muffins, chocolate-covered peanut butter cups, or cream-filled cupcakes. Dr. Janssen approves of Zuleika's eating these occasional sweets because it means she is taking her worming medicine.

A Viper in a Tube

ONE OF THE MOST dangerous snakes in the world might be expecting babies, and reptile keeper Robin Greenlee needed to know for sure. When the Zoo received the poisonous South African rhinoceros viper from a snake breeder a month earlier, it had been told that the female snake would have babies very soon, and had planned to trade the young vipers to other zoos.

Because the viper had not gained any weight since she'd been at the Zoo, Robin called the veterinarians to see if something was wrong. They decided to X-ray her to make sure she was expecting babies after all.

When Dr. Mike Loomis arrived to take Robin and the viper to the hospital, Robin used a long-handled snake hook to load the poisonous snake into a wooden box. Dr. Loomis brought along a bottle of antivenin, which is an antidote to

38

counteract the viper's poison in case anyone was bitten.

Because handling a poisonous snake is extremely dangerous, Dr. Loomis depended on snake expert Robin to help him take the X-ray. Again using the snake hook, Robin got the viper to crawl into a clear plastic tube. The middle part of the snake's body was wider than the tube, so it could only crawl in partway. This was alright because the dangerous part of the snake, its head, was in the tube where it couldn't bite anyone.

While Robin held the 2½-foot-long snake in the tube on the X-ray table, Dr. Loomis shot the X-ray. After it was developed, Dr. Loomis studied it on a light board. He concluded that the rhinoceros viper was definitely not expecting babies. Now Robin knew why the new female viper had not gained any weight. The San Diego Zoo wouldn't have any baby vipers to trade to other zoos...at least not this time around.

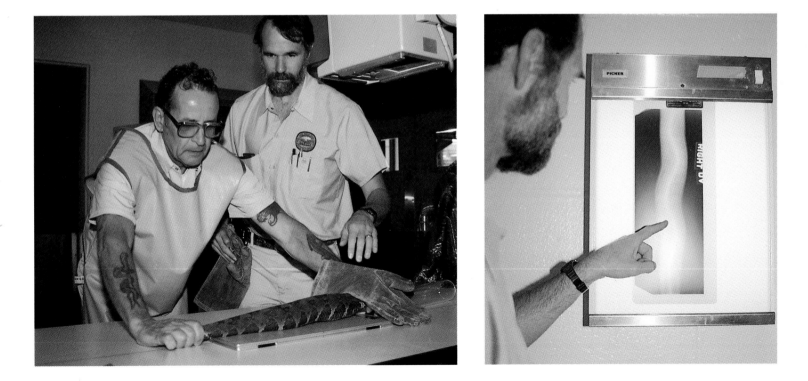

A Tufted Deer with a New Leg

O N A DECEMBER MORNING, one of the Zoo's rare Chinese tufted deer was found by her keeper with her left back leg caught in a chain link fence. Something may have frightened the tiny deer and caused her to run and jump higher than anyone thought she could. She leaped well above a protective barrier that cov-ered the bottom part of the fence, catching her leg in the chain link.

The keeper rushed her to the Zoo hospital. There, Dr. Mike Loomis anesthetized her and X-rayed her injured leg. What he found was a shattered bone and severely ripped muscles and tendons. The small deer's leg was so damaged that the only way Dr. Loomis could save her life was to amputate the lower part of her leg.

The surgery to remove her leg was successful, but the challenge would be to get the stump to heal. Dr. Loomis bandaged it, then put a cast over the bandage to pad and protect it. The deer would have to stay at the hospital until she recovered.

Every few days for several weeks, Dr. Loomis anesthetized the deer, examined her stump, and changed her bandage and cast. She was slowly healing but was having a difficult time keeping her balance as she tried to walk on three legs.

Dr. Loomis decided to try something that was rarely done for exotic animals. He would fit her with an artificial leg, called a prosthesis, to help her get around more easily.

The deer was anesthetized by Dr. Loomis while Kel Bergmann, a man who specializes in making artificial limbs for humans, made a cast of her stump and measured her other legs so the new one would match them. Humans with artificial limbs can take them off at bedtime. The challenge here would be to develop a leg that could be left on the deer for long periods of time.

It took many months to develop a leg that fit the little deer just right. The first leg rubbed her stump too much, causing her wound to open again. After the stump healed, a second leg was developed that worked much better. Through all of this, the little deer was anesthetized every few

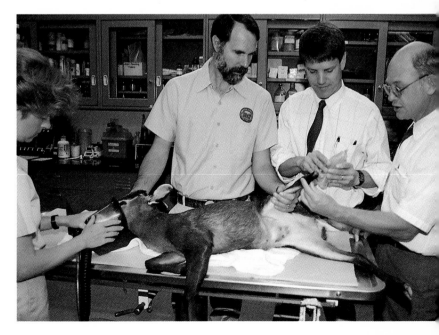

41

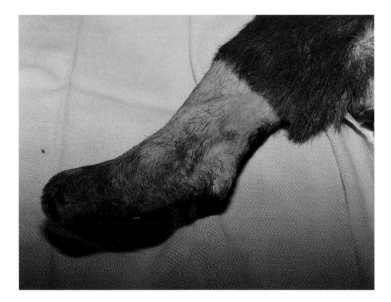

days so her stump could be checked and her bandages changed.

One June morning, while the little deer was still recovering at the Zoo hospital, Dr. Loomis had a big surprise when he came to work. The deer had become the mother of a five-pound female fawn! Dr. Loomis and the other veterinarians had had no idea the deer was pregrant. Even though she had been anesthetized and examined more than forty times, she had shown no signs of being pregnant.

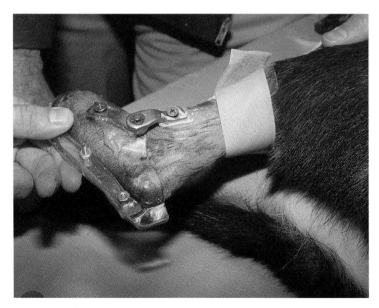

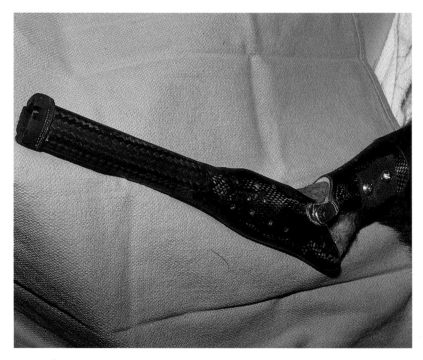

Normally, it is not safe to anesthetize a pregnant animal so often, but, fortunately, the baby was born healthy. If Dr. Loomis had known the deer was expecting a baby, he would have waited until she had given birth before fitting her with a new leg.

Dr. Loomis's treatment of the tiny tufted deer was certainly successful, though. Her injury was finally healed, she was walking well on her new artificial leg, and, perhaps best of all, she was being a caring mother to her newborn fawn.

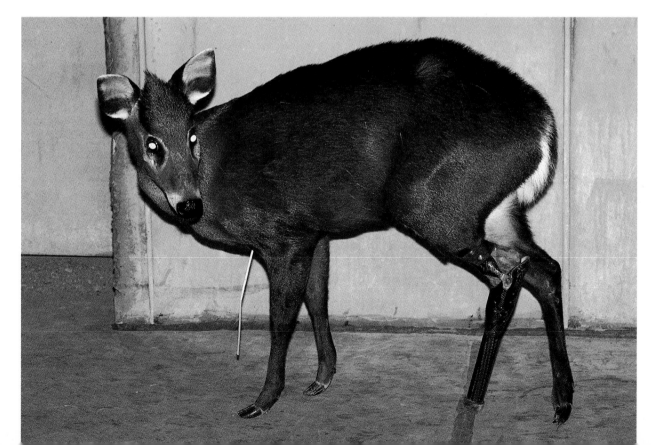

TO BE A VETERINARIAN

THE VETERINARIANS at the San Diego Zoo and the San Diego Wild Animal Park find their jobs extremely rewarding and satisfying. They care deeply about the animals, and are committed to wildlife conservation.

Becoming a veterinarian requires hard work, determination, and at least seven years of college study. If you want to be a veterinarian, whether it is for domestic or zoo animals, here are some steps that will help you prepare for veterinary school.

1. Get good grades in school now! There are fewer than thirty veterinary schools in the United States, and there are many students competing to get in. The higher your grades, the better your chances of being admitted.

2. Take as many high school courses as possible that are related to animals—such as biology, zoology, animal science, animal behavior, ecology, and botany.

3. Read magazines and books about animals and conservation.

4. Spend lots of time around animals by caring for pets and visiting zoos, wildlife sanctuaries, and county fairs.

5. Volunteer to work at your local humane society, animal rehabilitation center, zoo, pet store, veterinary office, dog obedience school, or other organizations that have something to do with animals.

6. Join work exploratory programs that relate to animals or clubs such as 4H, where you can gain practical, hands-on experience.

7. Be persistent and keep trying. Opportunities are out there; you just have to find them.

BIBLIOGRAPHY

Grahan, Ada and Frank J. *Wildlife Rescue.* New York: Cowles Book Company, 1970.

Herriot, James. *All Creatures Great and Small.* New York: St. Martin's Press, 1972.

Hodge, Guy R. *Careers Working With Animals.* Washington, D.C.: Acropolis Books Ltd., 1981

Livingston, Bernard. *Zoos: Animals, People, Places.* New York: Arbor House, 1974.

O'Connor, Karen. *Maybe You Belong in a Zoo: Zoo and Aquarium Careers.* New York: Dodd, Mead & Company, 1982.

Swope, VMD, Robert E. *Opportunities in Veterinary Medicine Careers.* Chicago: VGM Career Horizons/National Textbook Company, 1987.

Taylor, David. *Is There a Doctor in the Zoo?* Philadelphia and New York: J.B. Lippincott Company, 1978.

Taylor, David. *Zoo Vet: Adventures of a Wild Animal Doctor.* Philadelphia and New York: J.B. Lippincott Company, 1977.